Tower Air Fryer

Cookbook UK

A Variety of Delicious Tower Air Fryer Recipes
For Frying, Using European Units of Measure

Helen R. Somers

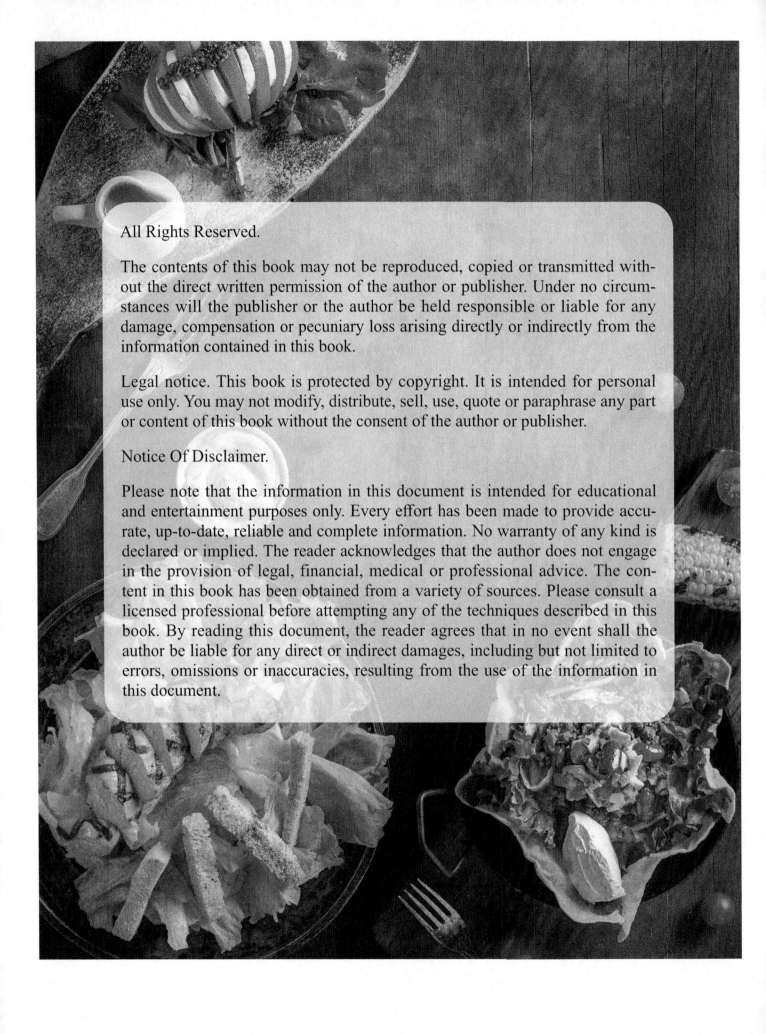

CONTENTS

Vegetable Side Dishes Recipes...39

Appetizers And Snacks Recipes..46

Desserts And Sweet Recipes 53

APPENDIX : Recipes Index...60

Introduction

This cookbook has been put together as a simple and understandable guide for you as you explore the use of a slow cooker. It is my goal that you will be able to make some lip-licking, drool-worthy but healthy meals while cooking with as little heat as possible.

I put in the effort to ensure that the ingredients used are very easy to find and the processes very easy to follow.

With this, I wish you a good time making dishes that will create lasting memories for you and your family

The air fryer can replace your oven, microwave, deep fryer, and dehydrator, and evenly cook delicious meals in a fraction of the time (and electricity costs) you're used to. Air frying makes it easy to feed your family healthy, irresistible meals with just five ingredients or less!

An air fryer can also help you succeed on the keto diet. Typically, fried foods are loaded with carbohydrates, so you might assume you have to avoid them altogether when on a keto diet. But when you use the air fryer, you can get the distinct crunch and mouthwatering taste of your fried favorites without the carbs. And you can choose your own low-carb breading! Another benefit to air frying is how much it shortens cooking time. This is especially crucial when you are hungry, short on time, and running low on supplies—a recipe for cheating on your diet. That's why your air fryer will be your best friend throughout your keto journey and help you stay on track, without venturing outside of a small list of ingredients and pantry staples.

Let's get air frying!

How Does the Tower Air fryer Works?

The technology of the Tower Air fryer is very simple. Fried foods get their crunchy texture because hot oil heats foods quickly and evenly on their surface. Oil is an excellent heat conductor, which helps with fast and simultaneous cooking across all ingredients. For decades cooks have used convection ovens to mimic the effects of frying or cooking the whole surface of the food. But the air never circulates quickly enough to achieve that delicious surface crisp we all love in fried foods.

With this mechanism, the air is circulated on high degrees, up to 200° C, to "air fry" any food such as fish, chicken or chips, etc. This technology has changed the whole idea of cooking by reducing the fat up to 80% compared to old-fashioned deep fat frying.

The Tower Air fryer cooking releases the heat through a heating element that cooks the food more healthily and appropriately. There's also an exhaust fan right above the cooking chamber, which provides the food required airflow. This way, food is cooked with constant heated air. This leads to the same heating temperature reaching every single part of the food that is being cooked. So, this is an only grill and the exhaust fan that is helping the Tower Air fryer to boost air at a constantly high speed to cook healthy food with less fat.

The internal pressure increases the temperature that will then be controlled by the exhaust system. Exhaust fan also releases extra filtered air to cook the food in a much healthier way. The Tower Air fryer has no odor at all, and it is absolutely harmless, making it user and environment-friendly.

Benefits of the Tower Air Fryer:

•Healthier, oil-free meals

•It eliminates cooking odors through internal air filters

•Makes cleaning easier due to lack of oil grease

•The Tower Air Fryer can bake, grill, roast and fry providing more options

•A safer method of cooking compared to deep frying with exposed hot oil

•Has the ability to set and leave, as most models and it includes a digital timer

The Tower Air fryer is an all-in-one that allows cooking to be easy and quick. It also leads to a lot of possibilities once you get to know it. Once you learn the basics and become familiar with your Tower Air fryer, you can feel free to experiment and modify the recipes in the way you prefer. You can prepare a vast number of dishes in the Tower Air fryer, and you can adapt your favorite stove-top dish, so it becomes air fryer–friendly. It all boils down to variety and lots of options, right?

Cooking perfect and delicious as well as healthy meals has never been easier. You can see how this recipe collection proves itself.

Cleaning Your Air Fryer

Before cleaning it, first ensure that your air fryer is completely cool and unplugged. To clean the air fryer pan you'll need to:

Remove the air fryer pan from the base. Fill the pan with hot water and dish soap. Let the pan soak with the frying basket inside for 10 minutes.

Clean the basket thoroughly with a sponge or brush.

Remove the fryer basket and scrub the underside and outside walls.

Clean the air fryer pan with a sponge or brush.

Let everything air-dry and return to the air fryer base.

To clean the outside of your air fryer, simply wipe with a damp cloth. Then, be sure all components are in the correct position before beginning your next cooking adventure.

Pantry Staples

Each recipe in this book has five or fewer main ingredients, but also included are some additional kitchen staples to help ensure that the tastes and textures of your meals come out perfect. I've identified six nonperishable pantry staples that you likely already have in your kitchen and that you'll want to have on hand when creating the recipes in this book. These staples are:

● All-purpose flour

● Granulated sugar

● Salt

● Ground black pepper

● Baking powder

● Vanilla extract

These must-haves were chosen for their versatility and frequent use not just in the recipes that follow but also in recipes you may collect online, at family gatherings and parties, and more. In each recipe in this book, you'll find a list of which of these staples you'll also need, so be sure to stock up on anything you may be running low on beforehand.

With this final information in hand, you are truly ready to get cooking. Throughout the following chapters you'll find plenty of delicious, five-ingredient recipes to suit all tastes. Use these recipes as your guide, but always feel free to season intuitively and customize dishes to your liking—just be aware that doing so will change the provided nutritional information.

Measurement Conversions

BASIC KITCHEN CONVERSIONS & EQUIVALENTS

DRY MEASUREMENTS CONVERSION CHART

3 TEASPOONS = 1 TABLESPOON = 1/16 CUP

6 TEASPOONS = 2 TABLESPOONS = 1/8 CUP

12 TEASPOONS = 4 TABLESPOONS = 1/4 CUP

24 TEASPOONS = 8 TABLESPOONS = 1/2 CUP

36 TEASPOONS = 12 TABLESPOONS = 3/4 CUP

48 TEASPOONS = 16 TABLESPOONS = 1 CUP

METRIC TO US COOKING CONVERSIONS

OVEN TEMPERATURES

120 °C = 250 °F

160 °C = 320 °F

180° C = 350 °F

205 °C = 400 °F

220 °C = 425 °F

LIQUID MEASUREMENTS CONVERSION CHART

8 FLUID OUNCES = 1 CUP = 1/2 PINT = 1/4 QUART

16 FLUID OUNCES = 2 CUPS = 1 PINT = 1/2 QUART

32 FLUID OUNCES = 4 CUPS = 2 PINTS = 1 QUART = 1/4 GALLON

128 FLUID OUNCES = 16 CUPS = 8 PINTS = 4 QUARTS= 1 GALLON

BAKING IN GRAMS

1 CUP FLOUR = 140 GRAMS

1 CUP SUGAR = 150 GRAMS

1 CUP POWDERED SUGAR = 160 GRAMS

1 CUP HEAVY CREAM = 235 GRAMS

VOLUME

1 MILLILITER = 1/5 TEASPOON

5 ML = 1 TEASPOON

15 ML = 1 TABLESPOON

240 ML = 1 CUP OR 8 FLUID OUNCES

1 LITER = 34 FL. OUNCES

WEIGHT

1 GRAM = .035 OUNCES

100 GRAMS = 3.5 OUNCES

500 GRAMS = 1.1 POUNDS

1 KILOGRAM = 35 OUNCES

US TO METRIC COOKING CONVERSIONS

1/5 TSP = 1 ML

1 TSP = 5 ML

1 TBSP = 15 ML

1 FL OUNCE = 30 ML

1 CUP = 237 ML

1 PINT (2 CUPS) = 473 ML

1 QUART (4 CUPS) = .95 LITER

1 GALLON (16 CUPS) = 3.8 LITERS

1 OZ = 28 GRAMS

1 POUND = 454 GRAMS

BUTTER

1 CUP BUTTER = 2 STICKS = 8 OUNCES = 230 GRAMS = 8 TABLESPOONS

WHAT DOES 1 CUP EQUAL

1 CUP = 8 FLUID OUNCES

1 CUP = 16 TABLESPOONS

1 CUP = 48 TEASPOONS

1 CUP = 1/2 PINT

1 CUP = 1/4 QUART

1 CUP = 1/16 GALLON

1 CUP = 240 ML

BAKING PAN CONVERSIONS

1 CUP ALL-PURPOSE FLOUR = 4.5 OZ

1 CUP ROLLED OATS = 3 OZ 1 LARGE EGG = 1.7 OZ

1 CUP BUTTER = 8 OZ 1 CUP MILK = 8 OZ

1 CUP HEAVY CREAM = 8.4 OZ

1 CUP GRANULATED SUGAR = 7.1 OZ

1 CUP PACKED BROWN SUGAR = 7.75 OZ

1 CUP VEGETABLE OIL = 7.7 OZ

1 CUP UNSIFTED POWDERED SUGAR = 4.4 OZ

BAKING PAN CONVERSIONS

9-INCH ROUND CAKE PAN = 12 CUPS

10-INCH TUBE PAN = 16 CUPS

11-INCH BUNDT PAN = 12 CUPS

9-INCH SPRINGFORM PAN = 10 CUPS

9 X 5 INCH LOAF PAN = 8 CUPS

9-INCH SQUARE PAN = 8 CUPS

Beef , pork & Lamb Recipes

Beef , pork & Lamb Recipes

Apricot Lamb Burgers

Servings: 4
Cooking Time: X

Ingredients:

- 500 g/1 lb. 2 oz. minced/ground lamb
- 50 g/⅓ cup dried apricots, finely chopped
- 1 teaspoon ground cumin
- ½ teaspoon ground coriander
- ¾ teaspoon salt
- 1 egg, beaten

Directions:

1. Combine all the ingredients together in a food processor, then divide into 4 equal portions and mould into burgers.
2. Preheat the air-fryer to 180ºC/350ºF.
3. Add the burgers to the preheated air-fryer and air-fry for 15 minutes, turning carefully halfway through cooking. Check the internal temperature of the burgers has reached 75ºC/170ºF using a meat thermometer – if not, cook for another few minutes and then serve.

Air Fryer Beef Tenderloin

Servings: 2
Cooking Time: 15 Mints

Ingredients:

- 454 g beef tenderloin
- ½ tbsp olive oil
- ½ tsp salt
- 1 tsp rosemary and thyme, (fresh or dried)

Directions:

1. Preheat air fryer to 360°F (180°C).
2. Mix sea salt, rosemary and oil on a plate.
3. Pat the beef tenderloin dry with paper towels. Place on plate and turn so that the oil-herb mix coats the outside of the beef.
4. Place beef tenderloin in the air fryer basket.
5. Set to cook in an air fryer for 15 minutes.
6. This should give you medium-rare beef. Though it is best to monitor the temperature with a meat thermometer to ensure that it is cooked to your liking. Cook for additional 5 minute intervals if you prefer it more well done.
7. Remove beef tenderloin from air fryer, cover with kitchen foil and leave to rest for at least ten minutes before serving. This allows the meat to finish cooking and the juices to reabsorb into the meat.
8. Carve the beef tenderloin thinly against the grain to serve.

Air Fryer Frozen Meatballs

Servings: 3
Cooking Time: 10 Mints

Ingredients:

- 454 g Frozen Meatballs
- oil spray , to coat the meatballs
- BBQ or Tomato Sauce, optional

Directions:

1. Cook Frozen – Do not thaw first.
2. Shake or turn as needed. Don't overcrowd the air fryer basket.
3. Recipe timing is based on a non-preheated air fryer. If cooking in multiple batches back to back, the following batches may cook a little quicker.
4. Recipes were tested in 3.7 to 6 qt. air fryers. If you use a larger air fryer, they might cook quicker, so adjust cooking time.
5. Remember to set a timer to shake/flip/toss as directed in recipe.

Air Fryer Lamb Steaks

Servings: 2
Cooking Time: 7 Mints

Ingredients:

- 2 lamb steaks
- ½ teaspoon ground black pepper
- ½ teaspoon kosher salt
- Drizzle of light olive oil

Directions:

1. Remove steak from the refrigerator an hour before cooking to allow it to reach room temperature before cooking.
2. Preheat air fryer to 400°F/200°C.
3. Mix salt and ground pepper on a plate.
4. Pat lamb steaks dry, then rub or spray with a little olive oil.
5. Press each side of the steak into the salt/pepper mix, then place in air fryer basket. ensure they are not touching.
6. Air fry lamb steaks for 5 minutes for medium-rare (9 minutes for well-done).
7. Use an instant-read meat thermometer to check the internal temperature - it should be 160°F/71°C for medium-rare, or 170°F/76°C or above for well done. Remove lamb steaks from the air fryer, cover with foil and leave to rest for 5 minutes before serving.

Air Fryer Rosemary Garlic Lamb Chops

Servings: 4
Cooking Time: 15 Mints

Ingredients:

- 567 g rack of lamb , about 7-8 chops
- 3 Tablespoons olive oil
- 2 Tablespoons chopped fresh rosemary
- 1 teaspoon garlic powder or 3 cloves garlic, minced
- 1 teaspoon salt, or to taste
- 1/2 teaspoon black pepper, or to taste

Directions:

1. Pat dry the lamb rack. Remove silver skin from underside of ribs if needed. Cut into individual chops.
2. In a large bowl, combine olive oil, rosemary, garlic, salt, & pepper. Add the lamb and gently toss to coat in marinade. Cover and marinate for about 1 hour or up to overnight.
3. Preheat the Air Fryer at 380°F/195°C for 4 minutes. Spray air fryer basket/tray with oil spray and place lamb chops in a single layer, making sure not to overlap the meat.
4. Air Fry at 380°F/195°C for 8 minutes, flip and air fry for another 3-6 minutes, or to your preferred doneness. Serve warm.

Air Fryer Orange Chicken From Frozen

Servings: 2
Cooking Time: 15 Mints

Ingredients:

- 10 ounces (240 g) Frozen Orange Chicken (about 2 cups worth)
- Sauce from the Packaged Frozen Orange Chicken

Directions:

1. Place the frozen orange chicken in the air fryer basket and spread out into a single even layer. No oil spray is needed. Set the sauce aside (do not sauce the chicken yet).
2. Place the frozen orange chicken in the air fryer basket and spread out into a single even layer. No oil spray is needed. Set the sauce aside (do not sauce the chicken yet).
3. Warm the orange sauce in microwave for 1 minute or on stovetop for 2-3 minutes on medium heat. Toss cooked chicken with sauce and serve.

Air Fryer Bacon-wrapped Asparagus

Servings: 4
Cooking Time: 10 Mints

Ingredients:

- 12 asparagus spears
- 12 slices bacon
- 1 tablespoon light olive oil

Directions:

1. Preheat air fryer to 200°C/400°F.
2. Trim any woody bits from the ends of the asparagus spears, then wrap each asparagus spear with bacon, wrapping tightly from the bottom towards the top.
3. Lightly brush or spritz the air fryer basket with oil (optional, but recommended if your air fryer is prone to sticking). Then place the bacon wrapped asparagus in the air fryer in a single layer. Try to ensure it is not touching.
4. Air fry the asparagus for 10-15 minutes flipping it over halfway through the cooking time if required for your air fryer.
5. Cook until the bacon is crispy.

Simple Steaks

Servings: 2
Cooking Time: X

Ingredients:

- 2 x 220-g/8-oz. sirloin steaks
- 2 teaspoons olive oil
- salt and freshly ground black pepper

Directions:

1. Bring the steaks out of the fridge an hour before cooking. Drizzle with the oil, then rub with salt and pepper on both sides. Leave to marinate at room temperature for 1 hour.
2. Preheat the air-fryer to 180°C/350°F.
3. Add the steaks to the preheated air-fryer and air-fry for 5 minutes on one side, then turn and cook for a further 4 minutes on the other side (for medium rare). Check the internal temperature of the steak has reached 58°C/135°F using a meat thermometer – if not, cook for another few minutes. Leave to rest for a few minutes before serving.

Teriyaki Steak Skewers

Servings: 4
Cooking Time: X

Ingredients:

- 4 sirloin steaks, diced into 2.5-cm/1-in. cubes
- sliced red chilli/chili, spring onion/scallion and coriander/cilantro, to garnish
- MARINADE
- 60 ml/4 tablespoons soy sauce (or tamari)
- 2 tablespoons runny honey
- 1 teaspoon unrefined sugar
- ½ teaspoon brown rice vinegar
- ½ teaspoon onion granules
- 1½ teaspoons freshly grated ginger
- 1½ teaspoons freshly grated garlic

Directions:

1. Make up the marinade by combining all ingredients in a jar and shaking vigorously.
2. Bring the steaks out of the fridge 30 minutes before cooking. Place in a bowl, cover with the marinade and leave to marinate at room temperature for the full 30 minutes.
3. Preheat the air-fryer to 180°C/350°F.
4. Thread the marinated steak pieces onto metal skewers and place these into the preheated air-fryer. Air-fry for 3–5 minutes, depending on how rare you like your steak. Serve immediately, scattered with sliced chilli/chili, spring onion/scallion and coriander/cilantro.

Garlic & Pepper Pork Chops

Servings: 2
Cooking Time: X

Ingredients:

- 2 x 250-g/9-oz. pork chops
- 1 tablespoon olive oil
- garlic salt and freshly ground black pepper

Directions:

1. Preheat the air-fryer to 180°C/350°F.
2. Rub the olive oil into each side of the chops, then season both sides with garlic salt and pepper.
3. Add the chops to the preheated air-fryer and air-fry for 10 minutes, turning them over after 4 minutes. Check the internal temperature of the chops has reached at least 63°C/145°F using a meat thermometer – if not, cook for another few minutes and then serve.

Air Fryer Sweet And Sour Pork Balls

Servings: 4
Cooking Time: 10 Mints

Ingredients:

- 500 g pork mince
- 2 green shallots, white section thinly sliced, green section thinly sliced diagonally
- 2 garlic cloves, crushed
- 2 tsp finely grated fresh ginger
- 1/4 tsp Chinese five spice
- 25g panko breadcrumbs
- 1 egg, lightly whisked
- Ground white pepper, to taste
- Sweet and sour sauce
- 185 ml sweetened pineapple juice
- 80 ml tomato sauce
- 2 tbsp rice wine vinegar
- 2 tsp soy sauce
- 2 tsp cornflour

Directions:

1. Place the mince, white section of the shallot , garlic , ginger , Chinese five spice , breadcrumbs and egg in a large bowl. Season with salt and white pepper. Use clean hands to mix until well combined. Shape 1/4 cupfuls of the mixture into 10 balls.
2. Spray meatballs and base of an air fryer basket with oil. Cook, in batches, at 180°C/350°F for 10 minutes until golden and cooked through.
3. Meanwhile, to make the sauce, place the juice , tomato sauce , vinegar and soy sauce in a large, deep frying pan. Cook, stirring, over medium-low heat until warmed through. Place the cornflour and 1 tbsp water in a small bowl and whisk until smooth. Add to the sauce mixture. Cook, stirring, until mixture just comes to a simmer and thickens.
4. Add meatballs to pan and gently toss through the sauce until coated. Sprinkle with the green section of the shallot to serve.

Poultry Recipes

Poultry Recipes

Air Fryer Hunters Chicken

Servings: 4-6
Cooking Time: 20 Mints

Ingredients:

- Spray oil
- 2 Chicken breasts
- 4 pieces of smoked streaky bacon
- 40 g grated cheddar or mozzarella / cheddar mix
- 50 ml BBQ sauce

Directions:

1. Season your chicken breasts well.
2. Lightly spray the chicken breasts with a little oil.
3. Cook at 200°C/400°F for 10 minutes.
4. Wrap each chicken breast with two pieces of streaky bacon.
5. Cook at 200°C/400°F for 6 minutes.
6. Spread on the BBQ sauce and add the grated cheddar carefully.
7. Cook at 200°C/400°F for another 4-5 minutes.
8. Check the temperature of your air fryer hunters chicken before serving, to ensure it is a minimum of 74°C/165°F internally.

Pizza Chicken Nuggets

Servings: 2
Cooking Time: X

Ingredients:

- 60 g/¾ cup dried breadcrumbs
- 20 g/¼ cup grated Parmesan
- ½ teaspoon dried oregano
- ¼ teaspoon freshly ground black pepper
- 150 g/⅔ cup Mediterranean sauce or 150 g/5½ oz. jarred tomato pasta sauce (keep any leftover sauce for serving)
- 400 g/14 oz. chicken fillets

Directions:

1. Preheat the air-fryer to 180ºC/350ºF.
2. Combine the breadcrumbs, Parmesan, oregano and pepper in a bowl. Have the Mediterranean or pasta sauce in a separate bowl.
3. Dip each chicken fillet in the tomato sauce first, then roll in the breadcrumb mix until coated fully.
4. Add the breaded fillets to the preheated air-fryer and air-fry for 10 minutes. Check the internal temperature of the chicken has reached at least 74ºC/165ºF using a meat thermometer – if not, cook for another few minutes.
5. Serve with some additional sauce that has been warmed through.

Air Fryer Chicken Parmesan

Servings: 4
Cooking Time: 10 Mints

Ingredients:

- 2 large boneless chicken breasts
- Salt
- Freshlyground black pepper
- 40 g plain flour
- 2 large eggs
- 100 g panko bread crumbs
- 25 g freshly grated Parmesan
- 1 tsp. dried oregano
- 1/2 tsp.
- garlic powder
- 1/2 tsp. chilli flakes
- 240 g marinara/tomato sauce
- 100 g grated mozzarella
- Freshly chopped parsley, for garnish

Directions:

1. Pat the skin of your chicken dry and using a knife make small holes all around the chicken.
2. In a blender combine all remaining ingredients and blend for three minutes. Pour half the jerk marinade over the chicken and massage it in. Refrigerate overnight.
3. When ready to cook, bring grill temperature up to 165°C/330°F. Place the chicken skin side down and close BBQ lid for 5-7 minutes until it starts to brown. Turn over and cook for the remaining 5-7 minutes. Repeat twice more until chicken is dark brown and cooked all the way through.
4. Move chicken to the sides of the grill and brush remaining jerk sauce on top. Close the lid and cook for a further 5-7minutes.
5. Remove from BBQ and leave chicken to cool for around 10 minutes. Either eat on the bone or chop the meat into smaller pieces and serve.

Air Fryer Cajun Chicken Recipe

Servings: 5
Cooking Time: 30 Mints

Ingredients:

- 640 g chicken mini fillets
- Cajun seasoning

Directions:

1. Add chicken to a bowl.
2. Add cajun seasoning and rub all over the chicken fillets.
3. Add your chicken mini fillets to the air fryer.
4. Cook on for 20 minutes, turning 10 minutes in.
5. Check the temperature before serving. Chicken should be at least 74°C/165°F internally before serving.

Air Fryer Whole Turkey With Gravy

Servings: 12
Cooking Time: 3 Hrs 15 Mints

Ingredients:

- 6.35 kg raw Whole Turkey
- 90 g/6 Tablespoons butter , cut into slices
- 4 cloves garlic , sliced thin
- 1 Tablespoon kosher salt, or to taste
- black pepper , to taste
- Olive Oil (or oil of choice), to coat turkey
- 360 ml chicken broth
- 95 g all purpose flour (for the gravy)

Directions:

1. Thaw your turkey completely on the inside cavity. Remove giblets and neck bones from the turkey cavity.Pat the turkey dry.
2. Tuck the butter slices and garlic in-between the skin and the turkey breasts. Rub olive oil over the turkey and season with salt and pepper.
3. Place the lower rack in the air fryer and spray with oil. Place the turkey breast side down in the air fryer. Pour 1/2 cup of broth over the turkey. Place the extender ring and lid on the air fryer.
4. Air Fry the turkey at 350°F/175°C for about 2 1/2 to 3 hours.Every 30 minutes, based with chicken broth
5. After cooking for 2 hours, take off the air fryer lid and extender ring. Lift the turkey out, flip to breast side up, and then place back into the air fryer. Baste the turkey and then place the extender ring and lid back on
6. Continue to Air Fry at 350°F/175°C until the turkey reaches an internal temperature of 165°F/70°C at the thickest parts of the thigh, wings and breast, and the juices run clear when you cut between the leg and the thigh. Let rest for about 15-20 minutes

Air Fryer Chicken Fajitas Recipe

Servings: 4-6
Cooking Time: 20 Mints

Ingredients:

- 640 g chicken mini fillets
- 3 mixed peppers
- 2 white onions
- Fajita seasoning

Directions:

1. Slice your bell peppers and onions.
2. Add your chicken breasts to a bowl.
3. Spread the fajita seasoning over the top of the chicken and then rub it across the breasts well.
4. Add the chicken mini fillets to the basket.
5. Cook at 200°C/400°F for 10 minutes.
6. Add the onion and peppers.
7. Cook at 200°C/400°F for another 10 minutes.

Air Fryer Chicken Wings With Honey And Sesame

Servings: 1-2
Cooking Time: 10-30 Mints

Ingredients:

- 450–500g /2 oz chicken wings with tips removed
- 1 tbsp olive oil
- 3 tbsp cornflour
- 1 tbsp runny honey
- 1 tsp soy sauceor tamari
- 1 tsp rice wine vinegar
- 1 tsp toasted sesame oil
- 2 tsp sesame seeds, toasted
- 1 large spring onion, thinly sliced
- salt and freshly ground black pepper

Directions:

1. In a large bowl, toss together the chicken wings, olive oil and a generous amount of salt and pepper. Toss in the cornflour, a tablespoon at a time, until the wings are well coated.
2. Air-fry the chicken wings in a single layer for 25 minutes at 180°C/350°F, turning halfway through the cooking time.
3. Meanwhile, make the glaze by whisking together the honey, soy sauce, rice wine vinegar and toasted sesame oil in a large bowl.
4. Tip the cooked wings into the glaze, tossing until they're well coated. Return to the air fryer in a single layer for 5 more minutes.
5. Toss the wings once more in any remaining glaze. Sprinkle with toasted sesame seeds and spring onion and serve.

Thai Turkey Burgers

Servings: 4
Cooking Time: X

Ingredients:

- 1 courgette/zucchini, about 200 g/7 oz.
- 400 g/14 oz. minced/ground turkey breast
- 35 g/½ cup fresh breadcrumbs (gluten-free if you wish)
- 1 teaspoon Thai 7 spice seasoning
- 1 teaspoon salt
- 1 teaspoon olive oil

Directions:

1. Coarsely grate the courgette/zucchini, then place in a piece of muslin/cheesecloth and squeeze out the water. Combine the grated courgette with all other ingredients except the olive oil, mixing together well. Divide the mixture into 4 equal portions and mould into burgers. Brush with oil.
2. Preheat the air-fryer to 190°C/375°C.
3. Add the turkey burgers to the preheated air-fryer and air-fry for 15 minutes, turning once halfway through cooking. Check the internal temperature of the burgers has reached at least 74°C/165°F using a meat thermometer – if not, cook for another few minutes and then serve.

Air Fryer Peri Peri Chicken

Servings: 4
Cooking Time: 30 Mints

Ingredients:

- 640 g chicken mini fillets
- Peri peri seasoning

Directions:

1. Add the chicken mini fillets to a bowl.
2. Add the peri peri seasoning and then massage it all over the chicken breasts.
3. Place the chicken fillets into the air fryer basket.
4. Cook for 20 minutes at 200°C/400°F, turning the chicken when the cooking time is 10 minutes in.
5. When cooking, if you overcrowd your air fryer basket then ensure that you give it a good shake at least every 5 minutes while cooking.
6. Check the temperature of your peri peri chicken before serving, to ensure it is 74°C/165°F internally.

Whole Chicken

Servings: 4
Cooking Time: X

Ingredients:

- 1.5-kg/3¼-lb. chicken
- 2 tablespoons butter or coconut oil
- salt and freshly ground black pepper

Directions:

1. Place the chicken breast-side up and carefully insert the butter or oil between the skin and the flesh of each breast. Season.
2. Preheat the air-fryer to 180°C/350°F. If the chicken hits the heating element, remove the drawer to lower the chicken a level.
3. Add the chicken to the preheated air-fryer breast-side up. Air-fry for 30 minutes, then turn over and cook for a further 10 minutes. Check the internal temperature with a meat thermometer. If it is 75°C/167°F at the thickest part, remove the chicken from the air-fryer and leave to rest for 10 minutes before carving. If less than 75°C/167°F, continue to cook until this internal temperature is reached and then allow to rest.

Air Fryer Chicken Breast

Servings: 2
Cooking Time: 10 Mints

Ingredients:

- 1 large egg, beaten
- 30 g plain flour
- 75 g panko bread crumbs
- 35 g freshly grated Parmesan
- 2 tsp. lemon zest
- 1 tsp.dried oregano
- 1/2 tsp. cayenne pepper
- Salt
- Freshlyground black pepper
- 2 boneless skinless chicken breasts

Directions:

1. Place eggs and flour in two separate shallow bowls. In a third shallow bowl, combine panko, Parmesan, lemon zest, oregano, and cayenne. Season with salt and pepper.
2. Working one at a time, dip chicken into flour, then eggs, and then panko mixture, pressing to coat.
3. Place in air fryer basket and cook at 190°C/375°F for 10 minutes. Flip chicken, and cook for another 5 minutes, until coating is golden and chicken is cooked through

Fish And Seafood Recipes

Air Fryer Crab Cakes

Servings: 6
Cooking Time: 5 Mins

Ingredients:

- 60 g mayonnaise
- 1 egg
- 2 tbsp. chives, finely chopped
- 2 tsp. Dijon mustard
- 2 tsp. cajun seasoning
- 1 tsp. lemon zest
- 1/2 tsp. salt
- 450 g jumbo lump crab meat
- 120 g Cracker crumbs (from about 20 crackers)
- Cooking spray
- Hot sauce, for serving
- Lemon wedges, for serving
- FOR THE TARTAR SAUCE
- 60 g mayonnaise
- 80 1/2 g dill pickle, finely chopped
- 1 tbsp. shallot, finely chopped
- 2 tsp. capers, finely chopped
- 1 tsp. fresh lemon juice
- 1/4 tsp. Dijon mustard
- 1 tsp. fresh dill, finely chopped

Directions:

1. Make crab cakes: In a large bowl, whisk together mayo, egg, chives, Dijon mustard, cajun seasoning, lemon zest and salt. Fold in the crab meat and the cracker crumbs.
2. Divide the mixture equally, forming 8 patties. You can refrigerate them for up to 4 hours if you're not ready to fry them. (Patties can also be frozen on a parchment-lined baking tray.)
3. Heat the air fryer to 190°C/375°F and spray the basket and the tops of the crab cakes with cooking spray. Place the crab cakes into the basket in a single layer. Cook until deep golden brown and crisp, about 12-14 minutes, flipping halfway through.
4. Meanwhile, make tartar sauce: Combine all of the tartar sauce ingredients in a bowl.
5. Serve the crab cakes warm with hot sauce, lemon wedges, and tartar sauce.

Cod In Parma Ham

Servings: 2
Cooking Time: X

Ingredients:

- 2 x 175–190-g/6–7-oz. cod fillets, skin removed
- 6 slices Parma ham or prosciutto
- 16 cherry tomatoes
- 60 g/2 oz. rocket/arugula
- DRESSING
- 1 tablespoon olive oil
- 1½ teaspoons balsamic vinegar
- garlic salt, to taste
- freshly ground black pepper, to taste

Directions:

1. Preheat the air-fryer to 180°C/350°F.
2. Wrap each piece of cod snugly in 3 ham slices. Add the ham-wrapped cod fillets and the tomatoes to the pre-heated air-fryer and air-fry for 6 minutes, turning the cod halfway through cooking. Check the internal temperature of the fish has reached at least 60°C/140°F using a meat thermometer – if not, cook for another minute.
3. Meanwhile, make the dressing by combining all the ingredients in a jar and shaking well.
4. Serve the cod and tomatoes on a bed of rocket/arugula with the dressing poured over.

Parmesan-coated Fish Fingers

Servings: 2
Cooking Time: X

Ingredients:

- 350 g/12 oz. cod loins
- 1 tablespoon grated Parmesan
- 40 g/½ cup dried breadcrumbs (gluten-free if you wish)
- 1 egg, beaten
- 2 tablespoons plain/all-purpose flour (gluten free if you wish)

Directions:

1. Slice the cod into 6 equal fish fingers/sticks.
2. Mix the Parmesan together with the breadcrumbs. Lay out three bowls: one with flour, one with beaten egg and the other with the Parmesan breadcrumbs. Dip each fish finger/stick first into the flour, then the egg and then the breadcrumbs until fully coated.
3. Preheat the air-fryer to 180°C/350°F.
4. Add the fish to the preheated air-fryer and air-fry for 6 minutes. Check the internal temperature of the fish has reached at least 75°C/167°F using a meat thermometer – if not, cook for another few minutes. Serve immediately.

Air Fryer Tuna Mornay Parcels

Servings: 2-3
Cooking Time: 30 Mints

Ingredients:

- 30 g butter
- 2 green shallots, thickly sliced
- 2 tbsp plain flour
- 310ml /1 1/4 cups milk
- 80 g/1 cup coarsely grated cheddar
- 185 g can tuna in oil, drained, flaked
- 120 g /3/4 cup frozen mixed vegetables (peas and corn)
- 2 sheets frozen puff pastry, just thawed
- 1 egg, lightly whisked

Directions:

1. Heat the butter in a medium saucepan over medium heat until melted. Add the shallot and cook, stirring, for 2 minutes or until soft. Add the flour and cook, stirring, for 1 minute. Gradually add the milk, stirring constantly, until smooth. Bring to a simmer. Cook, stirring, for 2 minutes or until thickened slightly. Remove from heat and stir in the cheese . Transfer to a large bowl. Set aside to cool until room temperature.
2. Add the tuna and frozen veg to the white sauce and stir until just combined. Cut each pastry sheet into 4 squares. Place 1/4 cupful tuna mixture into the centre of each square. Fold corners of pastry towards the centre to enclose the filling. Pinch to seal.
3. Preheat air fryer to 190°C/320°F for 2 minutes. Brush parcels with egg. Grease the base of air fryer basket with oil. Place 4 parcels into the basket and cook for 8 minutes or until light golden. Turn and cook for a further 3 minutes or until golden. Repeat with remaining parcels. Serve.

Air Fryer Fish

Servings: 2
Cooking Time: 10 Mins

Ingredients:

- 1 (450g) cod, cut into 4 strips
- Salt
- Freshlyground black pepper
- 65 g plain flour
- 1 large egg, beaten
- 200 g panko bread crumbs
- 1 tsp. Old Bay seasoning
- Lemon wedges, for serving
- Tartar sauce, for serving

Directions:

1. Pat fish dry and season on both sides with salt and pepper.
2. Place flour, egg, and panko in three shallow bowls. Add Old Bay to panko and toss to combine. Working one at a time, coat fish in flour, then in egg, and finally in panko, pressing to coat.
3. Working in batches, place fish in basket of air fryer and cook at 200°C/400°F for 10 to 12 minutes, gently flipping halfway through, or until fish is golden and flakes easily with a fork.
4. Serve with lemon wedges and tartar sauce

Panko-crusted Air Fryer Mahi Mahi

Servings: 4
Cooking Time: 15 Mints

Ingredients:

- 4 (4 ounce) mahi mahi fillets
- 2 tablespoons grapeseed oil
- 2 cups panko bread crumbs
- 1 teaspoon of everything bagel seasoning
- ½ teaspoon garlic salt
- ½ teaspoon ground turmeric
- ½ teaspoon ground black pepper
- nonstick cooking spray
- 1 teaspoon chopped fresh parsley
- 1 medium lemon, cut into 4 wedges

Directions:

1. Preheat an air fryer to 400°F/200°C for 5 minutes.
2. Meanwhile, place mahi mahi fillets on a platter and drizzle with grapeseed oil.
3. Mix panko, bagel seasoning, garlic salt, turmeric, and pepper together in a shallow dish. Dip each fillet into the panko mixture to coat, then place in a single layer in the air fryer basket. Spray with nonstick spray.
4. Cook in the preheated air fryer until fish flakes easily with a fork, 12 to 15 minutes, flipping halfway through.
5. Remove from the air fryer. Garnish with parsley and lemon wedges. Serve immediately.

Air Fryer Shake N Bake Style Fish

Servings: 4
Cooking Time: 10 Mints

Ingredients:

- 454 g white fish fillets (cod, halibut, tilapia, etc.)
- 125 g Ice water, beaten egg, milk, or mayo , to moisten the fish

Directions:

1. Preheat Air Fryer at 380°F/195°C for 4 minutes.
2. Cut fish fillets in half if needed. Make sure they are even sized so they'll cook evenly. Moisten the fish based on seasoned coating instructions . Coat with the seasoned coating mix.
3. Spray an air fryer basket/tray with oil or place a perforated parchment sheet in the air fryer basket/tray & lightly coat with oil spray
4. Place the coated fish in a single layer. Make sure the fish is not touching or the coating may flake off when you flip them. Lightly coat with oil spray.
5. Air Fry at 380°F/193°C for 8-14 minutes, depending on the size and thickness of your fillets. After 6 minutes, flip the filets. Lightly spray any dry spots than then continue cooking for the remaining time or until they are crispy brown and the fish is cooked through. Serve with your favorite dip: tartar sauce, mustard, aioli, etc.

Sea Bass With Asparagus Spears

Servings: 2
Cooking Time: X

Ingredients:

- 2 x 100-g/3½-oz. sea bass fillets
- 8 asparagus spears
- 2 teaspoons olive oil
- salt and freshly ground black pepper
- boiled new potatoes, to serve
- CAPER DRESSING
- 1½ tablespoons olive oil
- grated zest and freshly squeezed juice of ½ lemon
- 1 tablespoon small, jarred capers
- 1 teaspoon Dijon mustard
- 1 tablespoon freshly chopped flat-leaf parsley

Directions:

1. Preheat the air-fryer to 180ºC/350ºF.
2. Prepare the fish and asparagus by brushing both with the olive oil and sprinkling over salt and pepper.
3. Add the asparagus to the preheated air-fryer and air-fry for 4 minutes, then turn the asparagus and add the fish to the air-fryer drawer. Cook for a further 4 minutes. Check the internal temperature of the fish has reached at least 60ºC/140ºF using a meat thermometer – if not, cook for another minute.
4. Meanwhile, make the dressing by combining all the ingredients in a jar and shaking well. Pour the dressing over the cooked fish and asparagus spears and serve with new potatoes.

Air Fryer Spicy Bay Scallops

Servings: 4
Cooking Time: 10 Mints

Ingredients:

- 454 g bay scallops, rinsed and patted dry
- 2 teaspoons smoked paprika
- 2 teaspoons chili powder
- 2 teaspoons olive oil
- 1 teaspoon garlic powder
- ¼ teaspoon ground black pepper
- ⅛ teaspoon cayenne red pepper

Directions:

1. Preheat an air fryer to 400°F/200°C.
2. Combine bay scallops, smoked paprika, chili powder, olive oil, garlic powder, pepper, and cayenne pepper in a bowl; stir until evenly combined. Transfer to the air fryer basket.
3. Air fry until scallops are cooked through, about 8 minutes, shaking basket halfway through the cooking time.

Alba Salad With Air Fried Butterfly Shrimp

Servings: 2
Cooking Time: 6 Mints

Ingredients:

- 250 g Butterfly Shrimp
- 5 cups arugula
- 12 g/½ cup Kalamata olives, pitted
- 56 g/2 oz Roquefort, crumbled
- 1 pear
- 1 avocado
- 2 celery stalks
- 112 g/4 oz canned mushrooms, drained
- For the dressing:
- 3 tbsp olive oil
- 1 small garlic clove
- 1 tbsp freshly squeezed lemon juice or apple cider vinegar
- 1 tsp Dijon mustard
- ½ tsp kosher sea salt
- ¼ tsp freshly-cracked black pepper

Directions:

1. Place Gorton's Butterfly Shrimp on air fryer rack and air fry at 200°C/400°F for 11 – 13 minutes, until reaching an internal temperature of 145°C/300°For higher.
2. Chop pear, avocado, and celery stalk into bite-sized pieces.
3. Add arugula, Calamata olives, crumbled Roquefort, drained mushrooms, chopped pear, and avocado to a medium bowl.
4. For the dressing, finely chop garlic clove. Add all ingredients in a small bowl and mix with a fork or whisk.
5. Gently mix in the Alba Salad Dressing. Add the salad to a medium serving platter. Top with the air fried Butterfly Shrimp. Enjoy!

Servings: 3-4
Cooking Time: 20 Mints

Ingredients:

- 1 box Popcorn Shrimp
- 1 large or 2 small heads broccoli
- 1 tbsp olive oil
- 1/2 tsp salt
- 1/4 tsp pepper
- 85 ml orange juice
- 2 tbsp honey
- 2 tbsp soy sauce or coconut aminos
- 1 tsp minced garlic
- 1 tsp minced ginger
- 1 tsp sriracha or chili garlic sauce
- 1 tbsp cornstarch or arrowroot powder

Directions:

1. Toss broccoli crowns with olive oil, salt and pepper. Add to air fryer basket and air fry for 6 minutes at 200°C/400°F.
2. Remove broccoli from air fryer.
3. Cook the half of the bag of the Popcorn Shrimp in your air fryer at 200°C/400°F for 8 – 10 minutes, until reaching an internal temperature of 165°C/320°F or higher.
4. Make sauce by whisking together orange juice, honey, soy sauce, garlic, ginger, sriracha and cornstarch. Heat over low heat for 10-15 minutes, whisking occasionally until sauce thickens and becomes sticky.
5. Toss shrimp in about half the sauce to start. Add broccoli and toss to combine.
6. Serve with rice and the remaining sauce to dip or drizzle on top. Enjoy

Vegetarians Recipes

Vegetarians Recipes

Air Fryer Coconut Curried Cauliflower

Servings: 4
Cooking Time: 30 Mints

Ingredients:

- 3 tsp Keen's Traditional Curry Powder, plus ¼ tsp extra
- 1 tbsp garlic powder
- 2 tsp cooking salt
- 150 g /1 cup self-raising flour
- 270 ml can coconut cream
- 60 ml/¼ cup sparkling mineral water
- 1 egg
- ½ large cauliflower, cut into florets
- 200 g tub Greek-style yoghurt
- 2 tbsp mango chutney
- Fresh coriander leaves, to serve

Directions:

1. Whisk curry powder , garlic powder , salt and flour in a medium bowl. Whisk coconut cream, mineral water and egg in a separate medium bowl.
2. Working in batches, dip cauliflower florets in egg mixture, then coat in flour mixture, then re-coat in egg mixture and flour mixture, shaking off excess. Place in an air fryer, in a single layer.
3. Spray cauliflower florets with oil. Cook, in batches, at 200°C/400°F for 15 minutes, turning halfway through or until golden and tender.
4. Meanwhile, combine yoghurt , chutney and extra curry powder in a small serving bowl. Season.
5. Place cauliflower and yoghurt mixture on a serving plate. Sprinkle with coriander and ser

Cheese, Tomato & Pesto Crustless Quiches

Servings: 1–2
Cooking Time: X

Ingredients:

- 40 g/½ cup grated mature Cheddar
- 3 eggs, beaten
- 3 cherry tomatoes, finely chopped
- salt and freshly ground black pepper
- ½ teaspoon olive oil, to grease ramekins
- 2 tablespoons pesto

Directions:

1. Preheat the air-fryer to 180°C/350°F.
2. Mix together the cheese, eggs, tomatoes, salt and pepper in a bowl.
3. Grease the ramekins with the oil (and line with parchment paper if you wish to remove the quiches to serve). Pour the egg mixture into the ramekins.
4. Place the ramekins in the preheated air-fryer and air-fry for 10 minutes, stirring the contents of the ramekins halfway through cooking. Serve hot with 1 tablespoon pesto drizzled over each quiche.

Air Fryer Nashville Southern Fried Sandwich

Servings: 2
Cooking Time: 30 Mints

Ingredients:

- 2 Quon Southern Fried Burgers
- 1/4 cup mayonnaise
- 4 tsp apple cider vinegar
- 1 tsp grainy mustard
- 1 tsp honey
- 1 clove garlic, minced
- 1/4 tsp each salt and pepper
- 1 cup packed shredded kale leaves
- 1/4 cup sriracha sauce
- 2 soft bread buns, toasted
- 8 gherkins, sliced

Directions:

1. Set air fryer to 200°C/400°F according to manufacturer's instructions. Generously grease air fryer basket. Place Quorn Southern Fried Burgers in an air fryer basket. Fry, turning after 5 minutes, for 10 to 12 minutes or until golden brown.
2. Meanwhile, make the kale slaw by stirring together the mayonnaise, vinegar, mustard, honey, garlic, salt and pepper; toss with kale until well coated.
3. Just before serving, toss burgers with sriracha. Assemble in bread buns with kale slaw and gherkins.

Air Fryer Potatoes And Onions

Servings: 4
Cooking Time: 20 Mints

Ingredients:

- 908 g russet potatoes
- 2 medium red onions
- 3 tablespoons light olive oil
- 1 teaspoon fine sea salt

Directions:

1. Peel the potatoes, cut into 1-inch cubes, and place into a bowl of cold water to soak for at least 5 minutes.
2. Peel the onions, cut into quarters lengthwise, then cut each quarter in half through the middle.
3. Preheat air fryer to 180°C/350°F.
4. Drain the potatoes and pat them dry. Place the potato chunks and the onions into a large bowl, drizzle with oil, add the salt, and toss to coat.
5. Place the potatoes and onions in the air fryer basket and cook at 180°C/350°F for 20 minutes, shaking the basket to redistribute the potato cubes 1 or 2 times during the cooking time.
6. The potato cubes should be golden brown and the onions will be crispy. Air fry for additional 2-3 minute intervals if required.

Two-step Pizza

Servings: 1
Cooking Time: X

Ingredients:

- BASE
- 130 g/generous ½ cup Greek yogurt
- 125 g self-raising/self-rising flour, plus extra for dusting
- ¼ teaspoon salt
- PIZZA SAUCE
- 100 g/3½ oz. passata/strained tomatoes
- 1 teaspoon dried oregano
- ¼ teaspoon garlic salt
- TOPPINGS
- 75 g/2½ oz. mozzarella, torn
- fresh basil leaves, to garnish

Directions:

1. Mix together the base ingredients in a bowl. Once the mixture starts to look crumbly, use your hands to bring the dough together into a ball. Transfer to a piece of floured parchment paper and roll to about 5 mm/¼ in. thick. Transfer to a second piece of non-floured parchment paper.
2. Preheat the air-fryer to 200°C/400°F.
3. Meanwhile, mix the pizza sauce ingredients together in a small bowl and set aside.
4. Prick the pizza base all over with a fork and transfer (on the parchment paper) to the preheated air-fryer and air-fry for 5 minutes. Turn the pizza base over and top with the pizza sauce and the torn mozzarella. Cook for a further 3–4 minutes, until the cheese has melted. Serve immediately with the basil scattered over the top.

Air Fryer Spinach Dip

Servings: 8
Cooking Time: 40 Mints

Ingredients:

- 227 g cream cheese , (1 pkg) softened
- 156 g packed frozen spinach , thawed and water squeezed out
- 100 g grated parmesan cheese
- 224 g mayonnaise
- 75 g chopped water chestnuts , drained
- 80 g minced onion
- 1/4 teaspoon garlic powder
- 1 teaspoon black pepper

Directions:

1. Spray the baking vessel with cooking spray or olive oil. Combine all ingredients together in a bowl. Mix to completely combine. Add the dip mixture into the baking vessel(s).
2. Air Fry at 300°F/150°C for 20 minutes. After cooking for 20 minutes, stir the dip, and then continue Air Frying at 300°F/150°C for 10 minutes.
3. Stir the dip again. Increase heat to 340°F/170°C and then continue air frying for 5-10 minutes or until golden brown.If cooking anything less than the full volume of dip, cook for less time and keep checking until it's finished with a brown crust.Serve with celery and cucumber for a low carb, keto option.

Goat's Cheese Tartlets

Servings: 2
Cooking Time: X

Ingredients:

- 1 readymade sheet of puff pastry, 35 x 23 cm/14 x 9 in. (gluten-free if you wish)
- 4 tablespoons pesto
- 4 roasted baby (bell) peppers
- 4 tablespoons soft goat's cheese
- 2 teaspoons milk (plant-based if you wish)

Directions:

1. Cut the pastry sheet in half along the long edge, to make two smaller rectangles. Fold in the edges of each pastry rectangle to form a crust. Using a fork, prick a few holes in the base of the pastry. Brush half the pesto onto each rectangle, top with the peppers and goat's cheese. Brush the pastry crust with milk.
2. Preheat the air-fryer to 180°C/350°F.
3. Place one tartlet on an air-fryer liner or a piece of pierced parchment paper in the preheated air-fryer and air-fry for 6 minutes (you'll need to cook them one at a time). Repeat with the second tartlet.

Butternut Squash Falafel

Servings: 2
Cooking Time: X

Ingredients:

- 500 g/1 lb. 2 oz. frozen butternut squash cubes
- 1 tablespoon olive oil, plus extra for cooking
- 100 g/¾ cup canned or cooked chickpeas (drained weight)
- 20 g/¼ cup gram/chickpea flour
- 1 teaspoon ground cumin
- ½ teaspoon ground coriander
- ½ teaspoon salt

Directions:

1. Preheat the air-fryer to 180ºC/350ºF.
2. Toss the frozen butternut squash in the olive oil. Add to the preheated air-fryer and air-fry for 12–14 minutes, until soft but not caramelized. Remove from the air-fryer and mash the squash by hand or using a food processor, then combine with the chickpeas, flour, spices and salt. Leave the mixture to cool, then divide into 6 equal portions and mould into patties.
3. Preheat the air-fryer to 180ºC/350ºF.
4. Spray the patties with a little olive oil, then add to the preheated air-fryer and air-fry for 10 minutes, turning once (carefully) during cooking. Enjoy hot or cold.

Miso Mushrooms On Sourdough Toast

Servings: 1
Cooking Time: X

Ingredients:

- 1 teaspoon miso paste
- 1 teaspoon oil, such as avocado or coconut (melted)
- 1 teaspoon soy sauce
- 80 g/3 oz. chestnut mushrooms, sliced 5 mm/½ in. thick
- 1 large slice sourdough bread
- 2 teaspoons butter or plant-based spread
- a little freshly chopped flat-leaf parsley, to serve

Directions:

1. Preheat the air-fryer to 200ºC/400ºF.
2. In a small bowl or ramekin mix together the miso paste, oil and soy sauce.
3. Place the mushrooms in a small shallow gratin dish that fits inside your air-fryer. Add the sauce to the mushrooms and mix together. Place the gratin dish in the preheated air-fryer and air-fry for 6–7 minutes, stirring once during cooking.
4. With 4 minutes left to cook, add the bread to the air-fryer and turn over at 2 minutes whilst giving the mushrooms a final stir.
5. Once cooked, butter the toast and serve the mushrooms on top, scattered with chopped parsley.

Aubergine Parmigiana

Servings: 2-4
Cooking Time: X

Ingredients:

- 2 small or 1 large aubergine/eggplant, sliced 5 mm/¼ in. thick
- 1 tablespoon olive oil
- ¾ teaspoon salt
- 200 g/7 oz. mozzarella, sliced
- ½ teaspoon freshly ground black pepper
- 20 g/¼ cup finely grated Parmesan
- green vegetables, to serve
- SAUCE
- 135 g/5 oz. passata/strained tomatoes
- 1 teaspoon dried oregano
- ¼ teaspoon garlic salt
- 1 tablespoon olive oil

Directions:

1. Preheat the air-fryer to 200°C/400°F.
2. Rub each of the aubergine/eggplant slices with olive oil and salt. Divide the slices into two batches. Place one batch of the aubergine slices in the preheated air-fryer and air-fry for 4 minutes on one side, then turn over and air-fry for 2 minutes on the other side. Lay these on the base of a gratin dish that fits into your air-fryer.
3. Air-fry the second batch of aubergine slices in the same way. Whilst they're cooking, mix together the sauce ingredients in a small bowl.
4. Spread the sauce over the aubergines in the gratin dish. Add a layer of the mozzarella slices, then season with pepper. Add a second layer of aubergine slices, then top with Parmesan.
5. Place the gratin dish in the air-fryer and air-fry for 6 minutes, until the mozzarella is melted and the top of the dish is golden brown. Serve immediately with green vegetables on the side.

Baked Aubergine Slices With Yogurt Dressing

Servings: 2
Cooking Time: X

Ingredients:

- 1 aubergine/eggplant, sliced 1.5 cm/⅝ in. thick
- 3 tablespoons olive oil
- ½ teaspoon salt
- YOGURT DRESSING
- 1 small garlic clove
- 1 tablespoon tahini or nut butter
- 100 g/½ cup Greek yogurt
- 2 teaspoons freshly squeezed lemon juice
- 1 tablespoon runny honey
- a pinch of salt
- a pinch of ground cumin
- a pinch of sumac
- TO SERVE
- 30 g/1 oz. rocket/arugula
- 2 tablespoons freshly chopped mint
- 3 tablespoons pomegranate seeds

Directions:

1. Preheat the air-fryer to 180°C/350°F.
2. Drizzle the olive oil over each side of the aubergine/eggplant slices. Sprinkle with salt. Add the aubergines to the preheated air-fryer and air-fry for 10 minutes, turning halfway through cooking.
3. Meanwhile, make the dressing by combining all the ingredients in a mini food processor (alterantively, finely chop the garlic, add to a jar with the other ingredients and shake vigorously).
4. Serve the cooked aubergine slices on a bed of rocket/arugula, drizzled with the dressing and with the mint and pomegranate seeds scattered over the top.

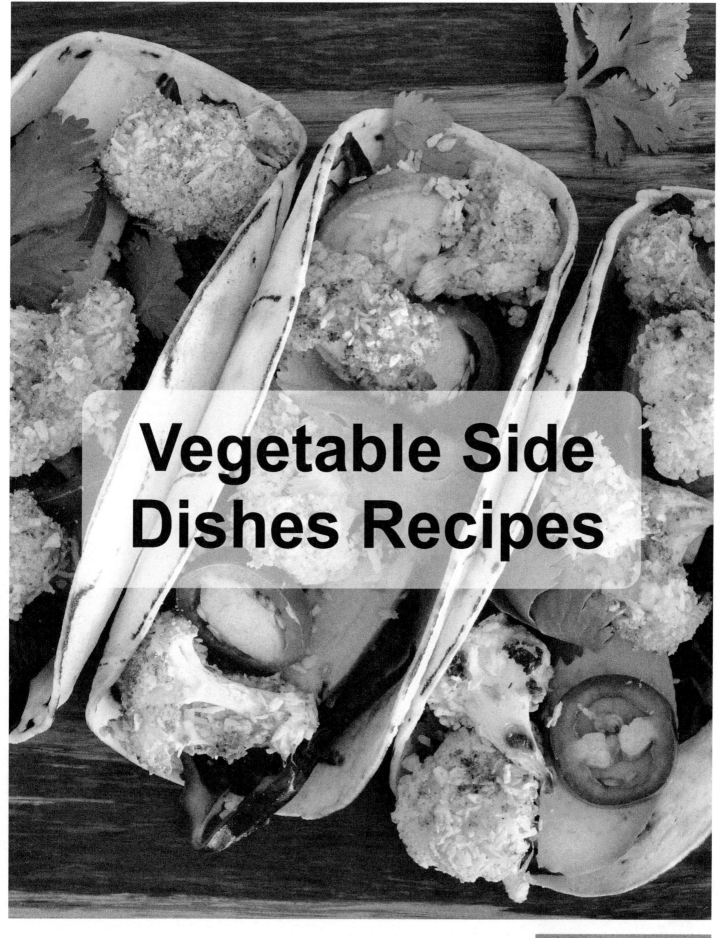

Vegetable Side Dishes Recipes

Vegetable Side Dishes Recipes

Crispy Broccoli

Servings: 2
Cooking Time: X

Ingredients:

- 170 g/6 oz. broccoli florets
- 2 tablespoons olive oil
- ⅛ teaspoon garlic salt
- ⅛ teaspoon freshly ground black pepper
- 2 tablespoons freshly grated Parmesan or Pecorino

Directions:

1. Preheat the air-fryer to 200ºC/400ºF.
2. Toss the broccoli in the oil, season with the garlic salt and pepper, then toss over the grated cheese and combine well. Add the broccoli to the preheated air-fryer and air-fry for 5 minutes, giving the broccoli a stir halfway through to ensure even cooking.

Air Fryer Roasted Tomatoes

Servings: 4
Cooking Time: 20 Mints

Ingredients:

- 8-10 tomatoes
- 15 ml vegetable oil
- 4 cloves of garlic (leave the skin on!)
- 10 sprigs of thyme
- 1 sprig of rosemary
- Generous pinch of salt and pepper

Directions:

1. Wash and dry tomatoes.
2. Place in a bowl with the vegetable oil and garlic cloves.
3. Mix well until all tomatoes are coated.
4. Add the herbs and salt and pepper.
5. Cook at 200°C/400°F for 20 minutes. Check at the 10 minute mark and shake gently if needed

Air Fryer Asparagus

Servings: 2
Cooking Time: 5 Mints

Ingredients:

• 1 bunch thick asparagus spears

Directions:

1. Preheat the air fryer to 180°C/350°F.
2. Place asparagus in the basket of the air fryer. Spray with oil. Season. Air fry for 4 minutes or until tender-crisp.

Butternut Squash

Servings: 4
Cooking Time: X

Ingredients:

• 500 g/1 lb. 2 oz. butternut squash, chopped into 2.5-cm/1-in. cubes
• 1 tablespoon olive oil or avocado oil
• 1 teaspoon smoked paprika
• 1 teaspoon dried oregano
• ½ teaspoon salt
• ¼ teaspoon freshly ground black pepper

Directions:

1. Preheat the air-fryer to 180ºC/350ºF.
2. In a bowl toss the butternut squash cubes in the oil and all the seasonings.
3. Add the butternut squash cubes to the preheated air-fryer and air-fry for 16–18 minutes, shaking the drawer once during cooking.

Yorkshire Puddings

Servings: 2
Cooking Time: X

Ingredients:

- 1 tablespoon olive oil
- 70 g/½ cup plus ½ tablespoon plain/all-purpose flour (gluten-free if you wish)
- 100 ml/7 tablespoons milk
- 2 eggs
- salt and freshly ground black pepper

Directions:

1. You will need 4 ramekins. Preheat the air-fryer to 200°C/400°F.
2. Using a pastry brush, oil the base and sides of each ramekin, dividing the oil equally between the ramekins. Place the greased ramekins in the preheated air-fryer and heat for 5 minutes.
3. Meanwhile, in a food processor or using a whisk, combine the flour, milk, eggs and seasoning until you have a batter that is frothy on top. Divide the batter equally between the preheated ramekins. Return the ramekins to the air-fryer and air-fry for 20 minutes without opening the drawer. Remove the Yorkshire puddings from the ramekins and serve immediately.

Asparagus Spears

Servings: 2
Cooking Time: X

Ingredients:

- 1 bunch of trimmed asparagus
- 1 teaspoon olive oil
- ¼ teaspoon salt
- ⅛ teaspoon freshly ground black pepper

Directions:

1. Preheat the air-fryer to 180°C/350°F.
2. Toss the asparagus spears in the oil and seasoning. Add these to the preheated air-fryer and air-fry for 8–12 minutes, turning once (cooking time depends on the thickness of the stalks, which should retain some bite).

Patatas Bravas

Servings: 4
Cooking Time: X

Ingredients:

- 750 g/1 lb. 10 oz. baby new potatoes
- 1 tablespoon olive oil
- ¼ teaspoon salt
- freshly chopped flat-leaf parsley, to garnish
- SAUCE
- 1 tablespoon olive oil
- 1 small red onion, finely diced
- 2–3 garlic cloves, crushed
- 1 tablespoon smoked paprika
- ¼ teaspoon cayenne pepper
- 400-g/14-oz. can chopped tomatoes
- 4 pitted green olives, halved
- ½ teaspoon salt

Directions:

1. Preheat the air-fryer to 200°C/400°F.
2. Rinse the potatoes and chop them to the same size as the smallest potato, then toss in the olive oil and sprinkle with the salt. Place the potatoes in the preheated air-fryer and air-fry for 18 minutes. Toss or shake the potatoes in the drawer halfway through.
3. While the potatoes are cooking, make the sauce. Heat the olive oil in a saucepan over a medium heat. Add the onion and sauté for about 5 minutes. Add the garlic, paprika and cayenne and cook for 1 minute. Add the tomatoes, olives and salt, plus 125 ml/½ cup water and simmer for about 20 minutes, until thickened. Purée the sauce in a blender or food processor.
4. Serve the potatoes in a bowl with the sauce poured over and the chopped parsley scattered over the top.

Airfryer Parsnips Recipe (honey Glazed)

Servings: 2-3
Cooking Time: 18 Mints

Ingredients:

- 250 g parsnips
- 15 ml honey
- Salt & pepper to taste

Directions:

1. Wash and peel your parsnips.
2. Slice them lengthways into 4 or 6 pieces, depending on the size and length of parsnips.
3. Drizzle over the honey.
4. Place your parsnips in your airfryer.
5. Cook at 200°C/400°F for approximately 18 minutes.

Air Fryer Cauliflower

Servings: 2-3
Cooking Time: 5 Mints

Ingredients:

- 2 tbsp. ghee or butter, melted
- 1/2 tsp. garlic powder
- 1/4 tsp. turmeric
- 1 small head of cauliflower cut into small florets
- Salt
- Freshlyground black pepper

Directions:

1. In a small bowl whisk together ghee, garlic powder, and turmeric. Place cauliflower in a large bowl and pour over the ghee mixture, tossing to coat until all the florets are tinted yellow. Season generously with salt and pepper.
2. Preheat air fryer to 190°C/375°F for three minutes. Add cauliflower to air fryer basket in a single layer and cook, tossing halfway through, until golden brown, 10 to 12 minutes

Air Fryer Blooming Onion

Servings: 2
Cooking Time: 15 Mints

Ingredients:

- 1 (about 250g) large brown onion
- 1 egg
- 60ml milk
- 50 g plain flour
- 1 tsp sweet paprika
- 1 tsp garlic powder
- 1 tsp onion powder
- Sweet chilli sauce, to serve
- Sour cream, to serve
- Chopped fresh chives, to serve

Directions:

1. Cut the pointed top end from the onion. Peel. Place, cut side down, on a board and make 10 cuts, from the top to about 1cm from the base. Gently loosen onion segments to make 'petals'.
2. Whisk the egg and milk in a jug. Combine flour , paprika , garlic powder and onion powder in a small bowl. Place onion in a bowl and sift over some flour mixture, filling any gaps. Shake off excess and reserve. Drizzle egg mixture over the onion and into the gaps. Sprinkle with remaining flour mixture. Spray with olive oil. Cook in an air fryer at 180°C/350°F, spraying with oil halfway through, for 15 minutes or until golden and crisp. Serve with sweet chilli sauce , sour cream and chives

Crispy Sweet & Spicy Cauliflower

Servings: 2
Cooking Time: X

Ingredients:

- ½ a head of cauliflower
- 1 teaspoon sriracha sauce
- 1 teaspoon soy sauce (or tamari)
- ½ teaspoon maple syrup
- 2 teaspoons olive oil or avocado oil

Directions:

1. Preheat the air-fryer to 180°C/350°F.
2. Chop the cauliflower into florets with a head size of roughly 5 cm/1 in. Place the other ingredients in a bowl and mix together, then add the florets and toss to coat them.
3. Add the cauliflower to the preheated air-fryer and air-fry for 12 minutes, shaking the drawer a couple of times during cooking.

Appetizers And Snacks Recipes

Air Fryer Pepperoni Pizza Egg Rolls

Servings: 3
Cooking Time: 30 Mints

Ingredients:

- 113 g pepperoni slices , chopped
- 112 g shredded mozzarella cheese
- 120 ml marinara sauce , plus extra for dipping
- 1 teaspoon dried Italian seasoning (or any combination of dried basil, oregano, thyme, rosemary, etc.)
- 75 g bell peppers , chopped
- 15 egg roll wrappers
- water , for sealing the wrappers
- oil spray , for coating the egg rolls
- 120-240 ml optional dipping sauce of choice , marinara, ranch, bbq sauce, etc.

Directions:

1. Add pepperoni, mozzarella cheese, sauce, Italian seasonings and bell peppers in bowl. Mix well.
2. Using egg roll wrappers or spring roll wrappers, add about 2 Tablespoons of the filling to each wrapper. Tuck and roll the wrapper around the filling (watch the video in the post above to see how to roll even and tight rolls). Brush the top corner of the wrapper with water to help seal the wrapper end, and then finish rolling the egg roll. Repeat all the egg rolls.
3. Brush or spray rolls with oil to coat. Place a single layer of egg rolls in the air fryer basket (cook in batches).
4. Air Fry 380°F/193°C for 12-16 minutes, flipping halfway through. Cook until the wrapper is crispy and browned. If you use the larger wrapper or if your wrappers are thicker cook a little longer so that all the layers can cook through to avoid being tough and chewy.
5. Allow to cool a little (the filling will be super hot right after cooking), and then serve with your favorite dipping sauce.

Cheese Scones

Servings: 12
Cooking Time: X

Ingredients:

- ½ teaspoon baking powder
- 210 g/1½ cups self-raising/self-rising flour (gluten-free if you wish), plus extra for dusting
- 50 g/3½ tablespoons cold butter, cubed
- 125 g/1½ cups grated mature Cheddar
- a pinch of cayenne pepper
- a pinch of salt
- 100 ml/7 tablespoons milk, plus extra for brushing the tops of the scones

Directions:

1. Mix the baking powder with the flour in a bowl, then add the butter and rub into the flour to form a crumblike texture. Add the cheese, cayenne pepper and salt and stir. Then add the milk, a little at a time, and bring together into a ball of dough.
2. Dust your work surface with flour. Roll the dough flat until about 1.5 cm/⅝ in. thick. Cut out the scones using a 6-cm/2½-in. diameter cookie cutter. Gather the offcuts into a ball, re-roll and cut more scones – you should get about 12 scones from the mixture. Place the scones on an air-fryer liner or a piece of pierced parchment paper.
3. Preheat the air-fryer to 180ºC/350ºF.
4. Add the scones to the preheated air-fryer and air-fry for 8 minutes, turning them over halfway to cook the other side. Remove and allow to cool a little, then serve warm.

Air Fryer Cornish Hens

Servings: 2
Cooking Time: 40 Mints

Ingredients:

- 2 Cornish game hens (about 1.5 lbs./680g each)
- 1 teaspoon garlic powder
- 1 teaspoon smoked paprika
- 1 teaspoon dried basil (or herbs of choice)
- 1 teaspoon salt
- 1 teaspoon black pepper
- oil spray

Directions:

1. In a bowl, combine seasonings (garlic powder, smoked paprika, basil, salt, and pepper).
2. Spray Cornish hens with oil to coat. Rub seasoning mix around the hens.
3. Spray basket/tray of air fryer with oil spray or line with a perforated silicone liner or perforated parchment paper. Lay hens breast side down in the basket/tray.
4. Air Fry at 360°F/182°C for 20 minutes then flip the hens.
5. Air Fry for another 12-18 or until internal temperature reaches 165°F/74°C.
6. Allow the hens to rest for 10 minutes before serving.

Air Fryer Bacon Wrapped Corn On The Cob

Servings: 2-4
Cooking Time: Mints

Ingredients:

- 2-4 ears fresh corn , shucked and cleaned
- 2-8 slices bacon , depending on how much corn & if you do double bacon or not
- salt , to taste
- black pepper , to taste
- oil spray or olive oil

Directions:

1. Cut ends of corn to fit into your air fryer basket/tray. Or for smaller air fryers, cut the corn in half.
2. Coat all sides of the corn with light oil spray (if you're using only 1 bacon strip/ear). If needed, make sure to spray the ends of the corn where it can often get dry.
3. Wrap bacon around the corn. Skewer one toothpick to secure each end of bacon to corn. Skewer the toothpick side-ways into the corn and bacon so it does't stick up too much. (see our photos for the technique). Season with salt and pepper to taste
4. For 2 corn – Air Fry at 380°F/193°C for 10 minutes. Flip the corn. Continue Air Frying for another 3-8 minutes or until bacon is crisp and corn is tender.
5. For 4 corn – Air Fry at 380°F/193°C for 10 minutes. Flip the corn. Continue Air Frying for another 6-10 minutes or until bacon is crisp and corn is tender.
6. Remove toothpicks before eating. Add butter if desired and enjoy!

Bocconcini Balls

Servings: 2
Cooking Time: X

Ingredients:

- 70 g/½ cup plus ½ tablespoon plain/all-purpose flour (gluten-free if you wish)
- 1 egg, beaten
- 70 g/1 cup dried breadcrumbs
- 10 bocconcini

Directions:

1. Preheat the air-fryer to 200ºC/400ºF.
2. Place the flour, egg and breadcrumbs on 3 separate plates. Dip each bocconcini ball first in the flour to coat, then the egg, shaking off any excess before rolling in the breadcrumbs.
3. Add the breaded bocconcini to the preheated air-fryer and air-fry for 5 minutes (no need to turn them during cooking). Serve immediately.

Air Fryer Frozen Texas Toast

Servings: 4
Cooking Time: 10 Mints

Ingredients:

• 4 Frozen Texas Toasts (Cheese or Garlic)

Directions:

1. Place the frozen Texas toast in the air fryer basket and spread in an even layer (make sure they aren't overlapping). No oil spray is needed.
2. CHEESE TEXAS TOAST: Air Fry at 340°F/170°C for about 7-10 minutes, or until the cheese is golden and the toast is heated through.
3. GARLIC TEXAS TOAST (NO CHEESE): Air Fry at 340°F/170°C for 5 minutes. Flip the garlic bread over. Continue to Air Fry at 340°F/170°C for another 1-5 minutes or until cooked to your desired golden crispness.

2 Ingredient Air Fryer Pizza

Servings: 2-4
Cooking Time: 10 Mints

Ingredients:

• 240 g/1 cup natural or Greek yoghurt
• 350 g/2 cups self-raising flour
• grated cheese
• pizza sauce/passata
• toppings of your choice (pepperoni, pineapple, peppers, chicken etc)

Directions:

1. Mix the self-raising flour and yoghurt together until a dough consistency has been formed.
2. Split dough in
3. Roll each one out on a floured surface.
4. Place on a bit of parchment paper in an air fryer basket and cook at 200°C/400°F for 8 to 10 minutes, turning over half way.
5. Take pizza out and add pizza sauce, grated cheese & any other toppings of your choice.
6. Return to the air fryer basket and cook for a further 3 minutes.
7. Repeat with the 2nd pizza.

Air Fryer Frittata

Servings: 2
Cooking Time: 10 Mints

Ingredients:

- Oil or butter to grease the pan
- 3 eggs
- 1/4 red pepper, diced
- 1/4 green pepper, diced
- 10 baby spinach leaves, chopped
- Handful of cheddar cheese, grated
- Salt and pepper to season, optional

Directions:

1. In a bowl beat the eggs. Season with salt and pepper if required.
2. Grease the pan with the oil or butter and place it in the air fryer. Switch to 180°C/350°F and allow to heat for a minute. Add the peppers and cook for 3 minutes.
3. Pour the spinach and egg mix in. Sprinkle the grated cheese across the top. Cook for a further 6 minutes, checking half way through to make sure it isn't over cooking

Air Fryer French Toast Sticks

Servings: 6
Cooking Time: 5 Mints

Ingredients:

- 2 large eggs
- 80 ml double cream
- 80 ml whole milk
- 3 tbsp. caster sugar
- 1/4 tsp. ground cinnamon
- 1/2 tsp. vanilla extract
- Salt
- 6 thick slices white loaf or brioche, each slice cut into thirds
- Maple syrup, for serving

Directions:

1. Beat eggs, cream, milk, sugar, cinnamon, vanilla, and a pinch of salt in a large shallow baking dish. Add bread, turn to coat a few times.
2. Arrange french toast in a basket of air fryer, working in batches as necessary to not overcrowd basket. Set air fryer to 190°C/375°F and cook until golden, about 8 minutes, tossing halfway through.
3. Serve toast warm, drizzled with maple syrup

Air Fryer Turkey Avocado Burgers

Servings: 4
Cooking Time: 15 Mints

Ingredients:

- 454 g ground turkey
- 2 cloves garlic , minced
- 1 Tablespoon Worcestershire , fish sauce, or soy sauce (fish sauce is our favorite)
- 1 teaspoon dried herbs (oregano, thyme, dill, basil, marjoram)
- 80 g minced fresh onion
- 1/2 teaspoon salt , or to taste
- Lots of black pepper
- oil spray , for coating
- BURGER ASSEMBLY:
- 4 Buns
- 1 avocado , sliced
- Optional: cheese, radish sprouts, lettuce, tomato, et

Directions:

1. Preheat air fryer at 380°F/193°C for 5 minutes.
2. In bowl, combine turkey, garlic, Worcestershire sauce (or fish sauce or soy sauce), dried herbs, onion, salt and pepper. Mix everything until just combined.
3. Divide and flatten into 4 patties about 4" wide. Spray both sides with oil. If you have a smaller air fryer, you'll have to cook in two batches.
4. Air Fry at 380°F/193°C for 10-12 minutes, flip after 6 minutes. Cook to your preference or until the internal temperature reaches 165°F/74°C. If your patty is thicker, you many need to cook for a few more minutes.
5. For Turkey Cheeseburgers: add the slices of cheese on top of the cooked patties. Air fry at 380°F/193°C for about 30 seconds to 1 minute to melt the cheese.
6. For best juiciness, cover the patties and let rest for 3 minutes. Warm the buns in the air fryer at 380°F/193°C for about 1 minute while patties are resting. Serve on buns, topped with 1/4 avocado and your favorite burger toppings

Air Fryer Turkey Melt Sandwich

Servings: 1
Cooking Time: 10 Mints

Ingredients:

- 2 slices bread
- Slices leftover turkey slices or deli meat
- 1 Tablespoon butter
- good melting cheese (American, Swiss, cheddar, Gruyere, etc.)

Directions:

1. Layer cheese and turkey slices in between bread. Butter outside of bread with butter. Secure the top slice of bread with toothpicks through the sandwich. Lay sandwich in an air fryer basket.
2. Air Fry at 360°F/180°C for about 3-5 minutes to melt the cheese.
3. Flip the sandwich and increase heat to 380°F/190°C to finish and crisp the bread. Air Fry at 380°F/190°C for about 5 minutes or until the sandwich is to your preferred texture. Check on the sandwich often to make sure it doesn't burn. Allow it to cool a bit before biting into the yummy grilled cheese sandwich

Desserts And Sweet Recipes

Desserts And Sweet Recipes

Banana Maple Flapjack

Servings: 9
Cooking Time: X

Ingredients:

- 100 g/7 tablespoons butter (or plant-based spread if you wish)
- 75 g/5 tablespoons maple syrup
- 2 ripe bananas, mashed well with the back of a fork
- 1 teaspoon vanilla extract
- 240 g/2½ cups rolled oats/quick-cooking oats

Directions:

1. Gently heat the butter and maple syrup in a medium saucepan over a low heat until melted. Stir in the mashed banana, vanilla and oats and combine all ingredients. Pour the flapjack mixture into a 15 x 15-cm/6 x 6-in. baking pan and cover with foil.
2. Preheat the air-fryer to 200ºC/400ºF.
3. Add the baking pan to the preheated air-fryer and air-fry for 12 minutes, then remove the foil and cook for a further 4 minutes to brown the top. Leave to cool before cutting into 9 squares.

Air Fryer Zucchini Parmesan Rounds

Servings: 4
Cooking Time: 8 Mints

Ingredients:

- 2 large zucchini
- 1 tablespoon olive oil
- 1 teaspoon garlic powder
- salt (to taste)
- pepper (to taste)
- 57 g/1/4 cup Parmesan cheese

Directions:

1. Slice the zucchini into ¼ inch rounds
2. Transfer to a large mixing bowl and drizzle with olive oil, garlic powder, salt, and pepper. Gently toss to combine.
3. Transfer to the air fryer and top with shredded parmesan.
4. Set your air fryer to 200°C/400°F for 5 minutes. After 5 minutes, open the air fryer and flip the zucchini, then sprinkle parmesan on the other side. Close the air fryer and cook for another 4-5 minutes.
5. The zucchini rounds are ready once the parmesan cheese is golden brown and the edges of the zucchini are crisp.

Air Fryer Caramello Danish

Servings: 4
Cooking Time: 10 Mints

Ingredients:

- 180 g block Caramello chocolate
- 1 sheet frozen puff pastry, thawed
- Thickened cream, to serve (optional)

Directions:

1. Place a pastry sheet on a flat working surface. Cut the pastry sheet in half. Place chocolate in the centre of one half of the pastry sheet. Brush the edges with a little cream. Place the other half of the pastry sheet on top. Brush with cream. Cut six 0.5cm to 1cm wide strips from the remaining half pastry sheet.
2. Working with 1 pastry strip at a time, place it over the chocolate, pressing gently to secure to the base piece of pastry. Repeat with remaining pastry strips to form a decorative pattern. Trim pastry, leaving a 1cm border around chocolate. Brush with cream.
3. Place in an air fryer and cook at 200°C/400°F for 10 minutes or until crisp and golden. Turn the air fryer off and let pastry sit for a further 5 minutes.
4. Cut into slices and serve with cream, if using

4-ingredient Nutella Air Fryer Brownies

Servings: 8
Cooking Time: 40 Mints

Ingredients:

- 150 g/1 cup plain flour
- 225 g/1 cup white sugar
- 3 eggs, lightly whisked
- 300 g/1 cup Nutella
- Cocoa powder, to dust (optional)

Directions:

1. Lightly grease a 20cm round cake pan. Line the base with baking paper.
2. Use a balloon whisk to whisk together the flour and sugar in a bowl. Make a well in the centre. Add the egg and Nutella. Use a large metal spoon to stir until combined. Transfer to the prepared pan and smooth the top.
3. Preheat the airfryer to 160°C/320°F . Bake the brownie for 40 minutes or until a skewer inserted in the centre comes out with a few crumbs sticking. Set aside to cool completely.
4. Dust with cocoa powder, if using, and cut into pieces to serve

Servings: 9
Cooking Time: X

Ingredients:

- BASE
- 60 g/5 tablespoons coconut oil
- 1 tablespoon maple syrup
- ½ teaspoon vanilla extract
- 180 g/1¾ cups ground almonds
- a pinch of salt
- MIDDLE
- 185 g/1⅓ cups dried pitted dates (soak in hot water for at least 20 minutes, then drain)
- 2 tablespoons almond butter
- 90 g/scant ½ cup canned coconut milk (the thick part once it has separated is ideal)
- TOPPING
- 125 g/½ cup coconut oil
- 4 tablespoons cacao powder
- 1 tablespoon maple syrup

Directions:

1. Preheat the air-fryer to 180°C/350°F.
2. To make the base, in a small saucepan melt the coconut oil with the maple syrup and vanilla extract. As soon as the coconut oil is melted, stir in the almonds and the salt off the heat. Press this mixture into a 15 x 15-cm/6 x 6-in. baking pan.
3. Add the baking pan to the preheated air-fryer and cook for 4 minutes, until golden brown on top. Remove from the air-fryer and allow to cool.
4. In a food processor, combine the rehydrated drained dates, almond butter and coconut milk. Once the base is cool, pour this mixture over the base and pop into the freezer to set for an hour.
5. After the base has had 45 minutes in the freezer, make the topping by heating the coconut oil in a saucepan until melted, then whisk in the cacao powder and maple syrup off the heat to make a chocolate syrup. Leave this to cool for 15 minutes, then pour over the set middle layer and return to the freezer for 30 minutes. Cut into 9 squares to serve.

Air Fryer Cheese Biscuits

Servings: 4
Cooking Time: 30 Mints

Ingredients:

- 115 g self-raising flour
- 55 g butter
- Pinch of salt
- 35 g grated cheddar cheese
- 75 ml semi-skimmed milk

Directions:

1. Rub together the self-raising flour and butter.
2. Add a pinch of salt.
3. Grate 35 g of cheddar cheese and add this to your dry mix. Combine.
4. Add the semi-skimmed milk and mix well.
5. Divide the mixture into 6.
6. Line the air fryer basket with parchment paper.
7. Drop the mixture inside the air fryer basket.
8. Cook at 200°C/400°F for 8-10 minutes.

Grilled Ginger & Coconut Pineapple Rings

Servings: 4
Cooking Time: X

Ingredients:

- 1 medium pineapple
- coconut oil, melted
- 1½ teaspoons coconut sugar
- ½ teaspoon ground ginger
- coconut or vanilla yogurt, to serve

Directions:

1. Preheat the air-fryer to 180°C/350°F.
2. Peel and core the pineapple, then slice into 4 thick rings.
3. Mix together the melted coconut oil with the sugar and ginger in a small bowl. Using a pastry brush, paint this mixture all over the pineapple rings, including the sides of the rings.
4. Add the rings to the preheated air-fryer and air-fry for 20 minutes. Check after 18 minutes as pineapple sizes vary and your rings may be perfectly cooked already. You'll know they are ready when they're golden in colour and a fork can easily be inserted with very little resistance
5. Serve warm with a generous spoonful of yogurt.

Air Fryer Lemon Drizzle Cake

Servings: 8
Cooking Time: 35 Mints

Ingredients:

- 150 g butter, softened
- 150 g/2/3 cup caster sugar
- 2 tsp finely grated lemon rind
- 1 tsp ground cardamom
- 3 Coles Australian Free Range Eggs
- 225 g/1 1/2 cups self-raising flour
- 210 g/3/4 cup honey-flavoured yoghurt
- Lemon zest, to serve
- Lemon icing
- 10 g butter, softened
- 160 g/1 cup icing sugar mixture
- 1 1/2 tbsp lemon juice

Directions:

1. Grease a 20cm (base measurement) round cake pan and line the base with baking paper. Use an electric mixer to beat the butter , sugar , lemon rind and cardamom until pale and creamy. Add eggs, 1 at a time, beating well after each addition. Stir in flour and yoghurt. Spoon into prepared pan. Smooth the surface.
2. Preheat air fryer to 180°C/350°F. Place the pan in the basket of the air fryer. Bake for 35 mins or until a skewer inserted in the centre comes out clean. Set aside in pan for 5 mins before transferring to a wire rack to cool completely.
3. To make the lemon icing, place the butter and icing sugar in a bowl. Stir in enough lemon juice to make a smooth paste.
4. Place cake on a serving platter. Drizzle with the lemon icing and sprinkle with lemon zest to serve.

Air Fryer Frozen Apple Pie

Servings: 2
Cooking Time: 12 Mints

Ingredients:

- 1 frozen apple pie
- To serve
- Vanilla ice cream or whipped cream

Directions:

1. Preheat the air fryer to 320°F/ 160°C.
2. Place frozen apple pie in air fryer basket [Note 1].
3. Air fry apple pie at 320°F/ 160°C for 20-25 minutes until golden brown and hot in the center.
4. Remove pie from air fryer and allow to cook slightly before serving. Serve with a scoop of vanilla ice cream . Enjoy!

Baked Nectarines

Servings: 4
Cooking Time: X

Ingredients:

- 2 teaspoons maple syrup
- 1 teaspoon vanilla extract
- 1 teaspoon ground cinnamon
- 4 nectarines, halved and stones/pits removed
- chopped nuts, yogurt and runny honey, to serve (optional)

Directions:

1. Preheat the air-fryer to 180ºC/350º F.
2. Mix the maple syrup, vanilla extract and cinnamon in a ramekin or shake in a jar to combine. Lay the nectarine halves on an air-fryer liner or piece of pierced parchment paper. Drizzle over the maple syrup mix.
3. Place in the preheated air-fryer and air-fry for 9–11 minutes, until soft when pricked with a fork. Serve scattered with chopped nuts and with a generous dollop of yogurt. Drizzle over some honey if you wish.

Air Fryer Cheesecake!

Servings: 6
Cooking Time: 15 Mints

Ingredients:

- 450 g Cream cheese
- 2 Eggs
- 112 g/½ Cup sugar
- ½ tsp Vanilla Extract
- 84 g/1 Cup Honey Flavoured Graham Crackers
- 2 Tbsp Unsalted Butter

Directions:

1. Cut out a piece of parchment paper to line the baking pan.
2. Melt the butter and mix in the Graham crackers. Spoon it into the lined baking pan and press down to form a crust.
3. Place the baking pan into the air fryer basket and bake for 5 minutes at 180°C/350°F
4. While the crust is busy forming, blend the cream cheese and the sugar. Add one egg at a time, while mixing, until creamy, then add the vanilla and mix well.
5. Remove the basket from the air fryer and pour the cream cheese mixture into the graham cracker crust.
6. Place it back into the basket, adjust the temperature to 155°C/300°F and bake for 15 minutes.
7. After baking, remove it from the machine and let it cool on the counter before chilling in the fridge for 3 hours.
8. Spoon over any flavoured fruit coulis

APPENDIX : Recipes Index

Printed in Great Britain
by Amazon